Written by
Paul Goddard

Illustrated by
Martin Chatterton

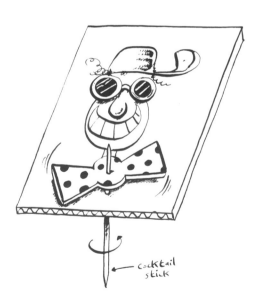

cocktail
stick

BBC CHILDREN'S BOOKS

This book is based on the BBC TV series *Bitsa*,
produced by Peter Charlton
and directed by Brian Jameson.

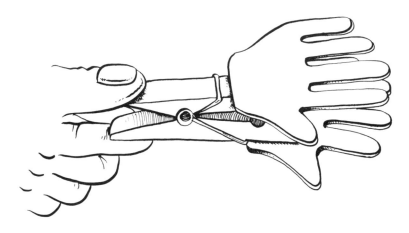

Published by BBC Children's Books,
a division of BBC Enterprises Limited,
Woodlands, 80 Wood Lane, London W12 0TT

First published 1993

Text © Paul Goddard 1993

Illustrations by Martin Chatterton
© BBC Children's Books 1993

ISBN 0 563 40328 4

Typeset by BBC Children's Books
Printed and bound in Great Britain
by Ebenezer Baylis, Worcester
Cover printed by Clays Ltd, St Ives plc

Contents

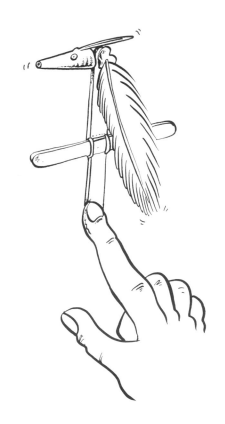

Handy Hints

Take care of your tools. Store them in a safe place, away from small children. If you ever have any doubts about how to use any of them, always ask an adult to give you a hand.

Cutting

Scissors
For paper and card.

Craft Knives
A sharp knife is very useful, and it's safe if used properly.
● Always cover the blade when you're not working.
● Always cut away from your fingers and body.
● Don't use too much force. A sharp blade is actually safer than a blunt one.
● Cut on an old, flat board – not your mum's best table!

Pliers
For wire.

Junior hacksaw
For bamboo and garden sticks. Hold them in a vice to keep them steady when you saw.

Making Holes

Use the point of a compass, or punch holes with a light hammer and nail. Mind your fingers, and put plenty of scrap card underneath.

Gluing and Taping

● Glue sticks are clean and good for paper.

● PVA and latex glues are best for cardboard.

● Use watered-down PVA to make papier mâché.

● Always leave plenty time for the glue to dry.

● Lots of bitsas also use clear sticky tape or modelling glue.

INTO THE WORKSHOP...

You can use all sorts of junk to create interesting models. Keep on the lookout for bits you could use, and then store them in a large cardboard bitsa box. (All sorts of things might come in handy, but make sure it really is junk — not just old biscuits or your auntie's best hat!)

Study the instructions first — you don't always need the exact bits, but you might need substitutes instead.

Above all, BE CAREFUL with tools and keep them in a safe place. Never fool around with tools.

Experiment, use your imagination and have fun making up new ideas of your own. Remember, if it's not a masterpiece, you can always say, 'Well, IT'S A BITSA!'

Painting

● Use water-based paint (like poster paint) for paper and card.

● You need oil-based paint (like enamel paint) for plastic, but it's expensive, so try to cover plastic with paper instead.

● For large bits of card, ask an adult if they have any left-over wall paints. Always clean your brushes after use.

Whoopee Cushion

plastic washing-up bottle

clothes peg

balloon

1 Wash and dry a plastic washing-up bottle. Remove the top.

2 Take a balloon, snip off the top and stretch the narrow opening over the end of the bottle.

3 To get a good raspberry sound, clip a clothes peg to the open end of the balloon. You may have to experiment with the position to get the best sound.

6

PARP!

Whoopee!

Place the bottle on a hard chair hidden under a comic or a piece of cloth and ask a friend to sit down.

squashed bottle

Excuse me! comic

Switchabods

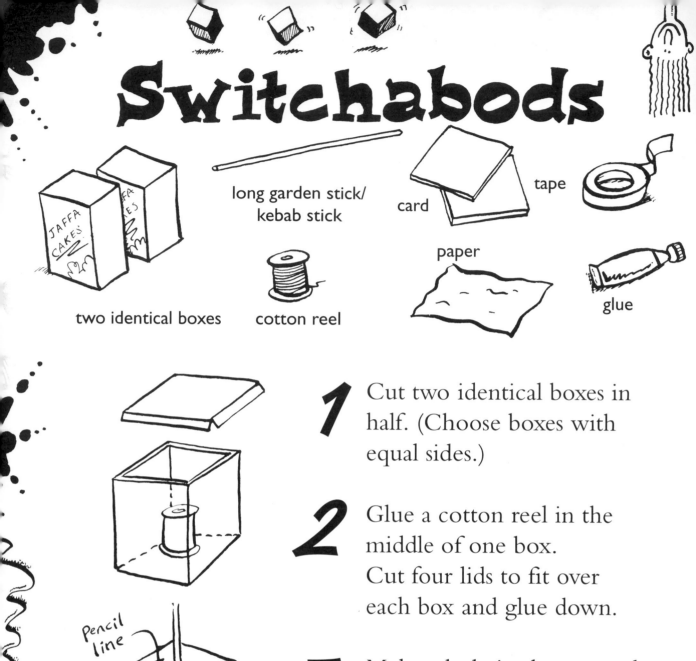

two identical boxes

long garden stick/ kebab stick

card

tape

cotton reel

paper

glue

Pencil line

1 Cut two identical boxes in half. (Choose boxes with equal sides.)

2 Glue a cotton reel in the middle of one box.
Cut four lids to fit over each box and glue down.

3 Make a hole in the top and bottom of each box, large enough to fit a long garden stick. (Find the centre by drawing a line from corner to corner.)
Fit the stick into the cotton reel and slide on the boxes.

4 Decide on four crazy characters, one for each side – perhaps a medieval knight, a monster, a clown or even your sister!

Draw the head on the top box, then the body, next the legs and finally the feet on the bottom box.

Bitsa Tip

You might find it easier to draw the characters out first on paper, then glue them onto the sides.

Bodyswop

By revolving each box you should get some extraordinary characters.

Have you even seen your sister with the body of a sumo wrestler and webbed feet?

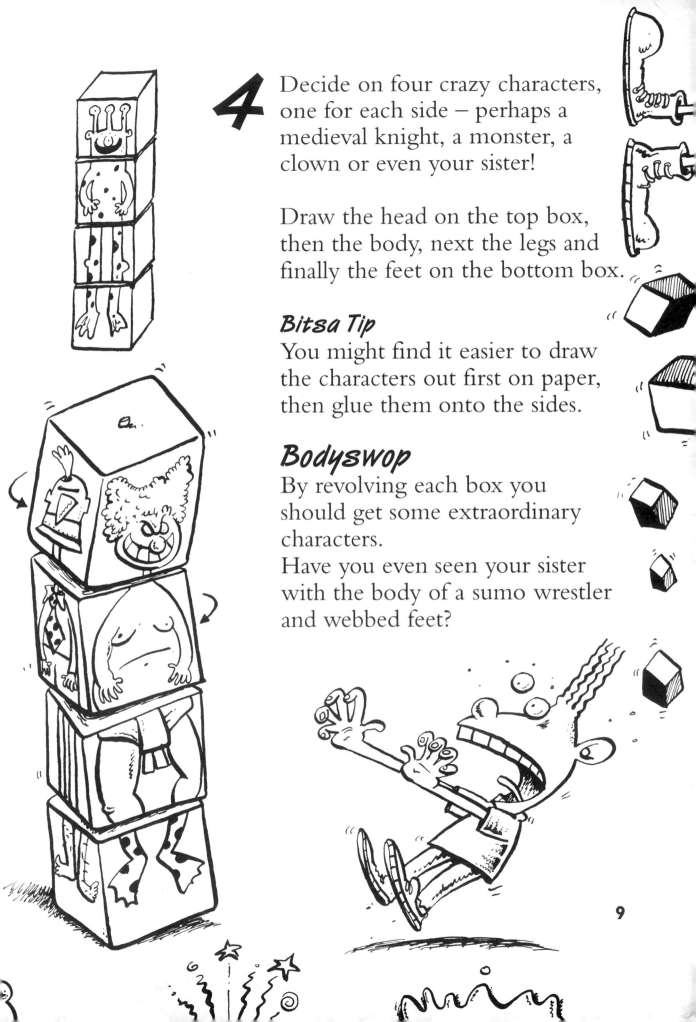

Rock 'n' Roll Ducks

small sweet box

thin cardboard

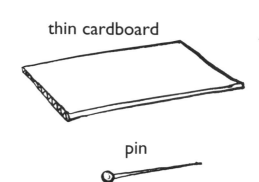

tape

Plasticine

pin

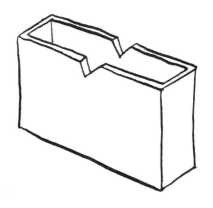

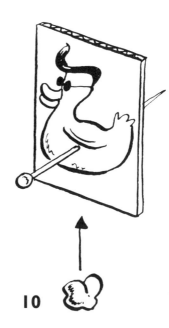

1 Cut off the long narrow side of a small sweet box.
Snip out two 'V' shaped slits opposite one another along the edges.

2 Cut out a piece of cardboard one-and-a-half times the height of your box and quite a bit smaller than its length.
Draw on a picture of a duck.
Push a pin through, one third of the way up.

3 Attach a small piece of Plasticine to the bottom of the cardboard, directly below the pin.

4 Rest the pin in the 'V' slits, checking that the card is free to rock back and forth by adjusting the size of the Plasticine.
Tape a narrow strip of card to the bottom of the box.

Ducking and Diving

By moving the strip of card back and forth, the duck will begin to rock. Make a drake and ducklings and have a group of rockers.

Other Possible Rockers

Pirate ships, eyeballs, horses, your Maths teacher.

Heartbeat

red plastic bag

bendy straws

small box

tape

crisp packet

old sponge

1 Cut out two identical hearts from a red plastic bag.

2 Tape a straw in the centre of one heart and lay the other heart on top.
Carefully seal all round the edges with tape.

3 Fit the heart into a small box with the straw going out through a hole in the back. (You might have to glue in a false bottom so the heart sits just below the lid.)

hole

false bottom

tape

12

4 To make your heart beat use an empty crisp packet.
Snip off the top to make a clean straight edge.
Fill the bag with a piece of sponge, fit in one end of a bendy straw and seal up the bag with tape.

5 Join the two straws together by cutting a slit in one end and inserting it in the other.

Beating Instructions

By squeezing and releasing the crisp bag your heart will beat for the 'one you love' or faster and slower if your favourite film star or heart-throb appears on TV.

squeeze bag to pump heart

Hide and Seek

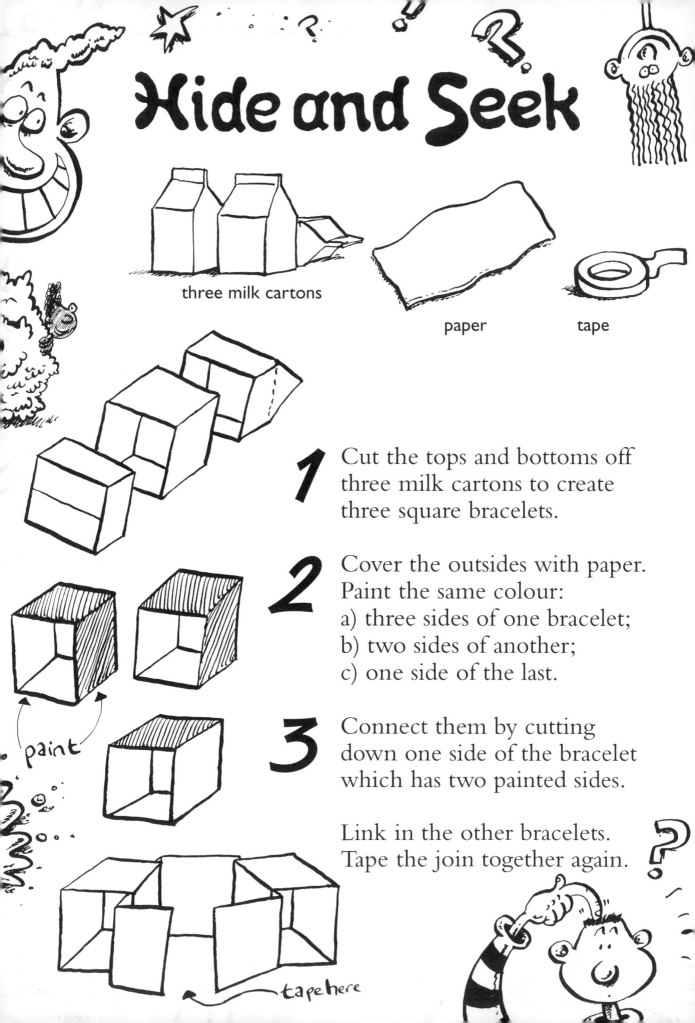

three milk cartons

paper

tape

1 Cut the tops and bottoms off three milk cartons to create three square bracelets.

2 Cover the outsides with paper. Paint the same colour:
a) three sides of one bracelet;
b) two sides of another;
c) one side of the last.

paint

3 Connect them by cutting down one side of the bracelet which has two painted sides.

Link in the other bracelets. Tape the join together again.

tape here

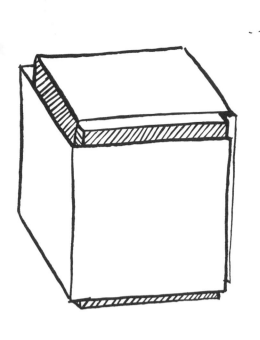

The Puzzle

It will now be possible to make the bracelets slot into each other to form a single cube.

However, it's not quite so simple to get all the plain sides facing out or all the painted sides facing in.

Hide and Seek

Draw different fruits on the plain sides – then switch the bracelets so you can't see the drawings and ask a friend to seek out the hidden fruits.

How long will it take to hide them again?

Hide and seek planets, pop stars or secret messages.

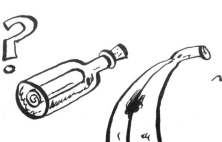

LEAPFROGS

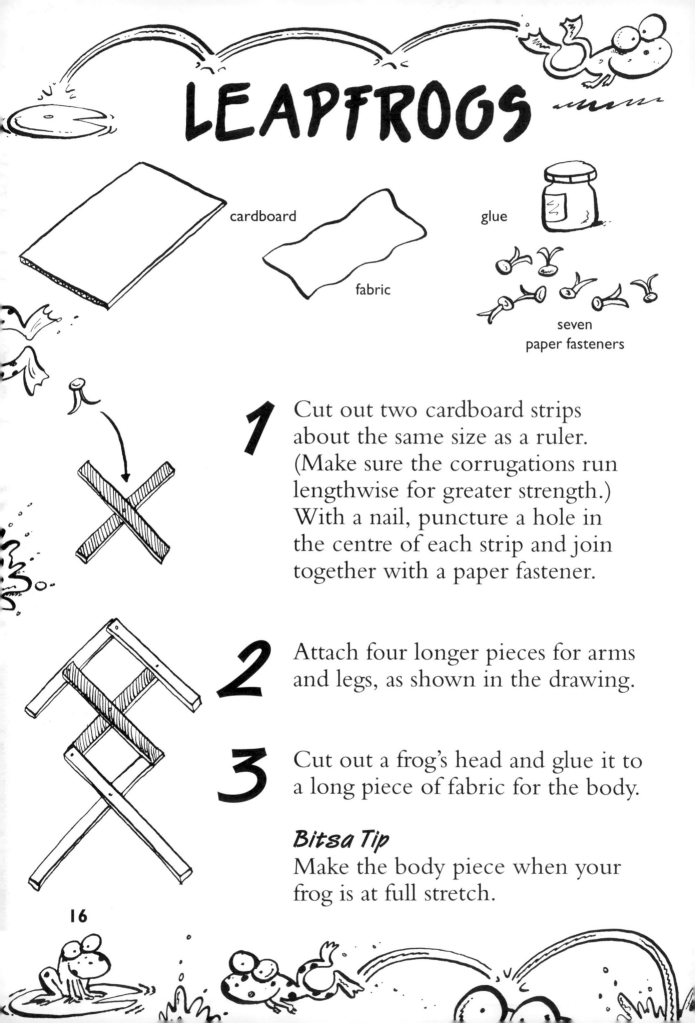

cardboard

fabric

glue

seven
paper fasteners

1 Cut out two cardboard strips about the same size as a ruler. (Make sure the corrugations run lengthwise for greater strength.) With a nail, puncture a hole in the centre of each strip and join together with a paper fastener.

2 Attach four longer pieces for arms and legs, as shown in the drawing.

3 Cut out a frog's head and glue it to a long piece of fabric for the body.

Bitsa Tip
Make the body piece when your frog is at full stretch.

glue material to head

fasten fabric here

4 Fit the head onto the top fastener and the bottom of the material to the centre fastener.

By pulling the legs together your frog will leap like a prima ballerina.

Groovy Ghosts

Make ghosts that leap up from behind chairs to scare your friends.

HANDS' BOOGIE

Handshaker
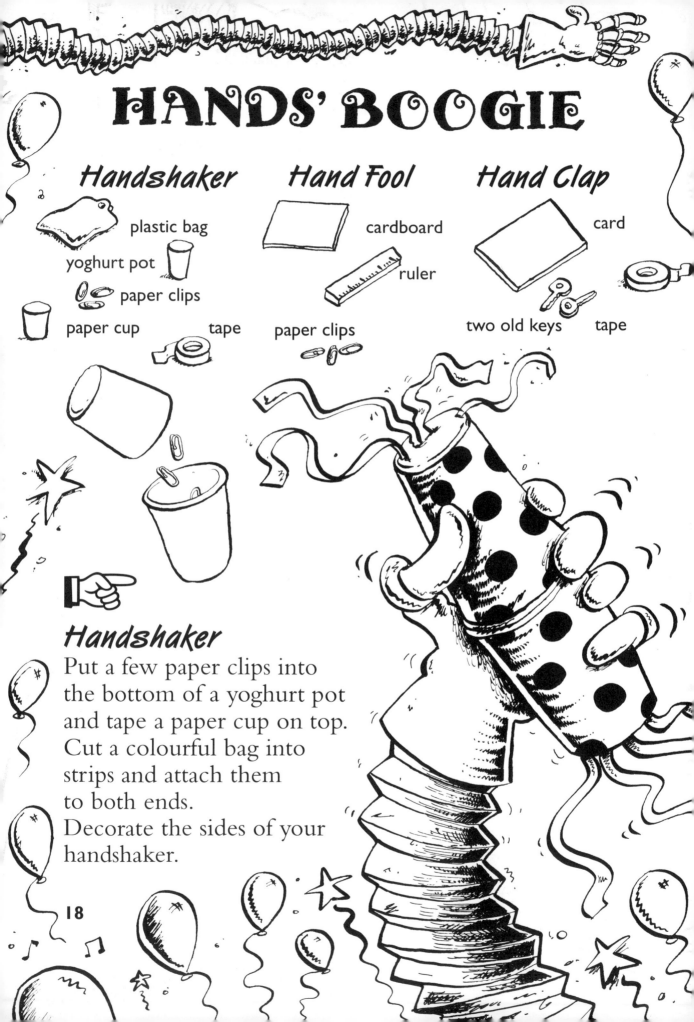
plastic bag
yoghurt pot
paper clips
paper cup
tape

Hand Fool
cardboard
ruler
paper clips

Hand Clap
card
two old keys
tape

Handshaker

Put a few paper clips into the bottom of a yoghurt pot and tape a paper cup on top. Cut a colourful bag into strips and attach them to both ends. Decorate the sides of your handshaker.

18

Hand Fool

Tape a ruler to the back of a small piece of cardboard.

For each leg join three paper clips together. Push them into the corrugated end of the cardboard.

Draw on your favourite dancer or fool.

fold

ape

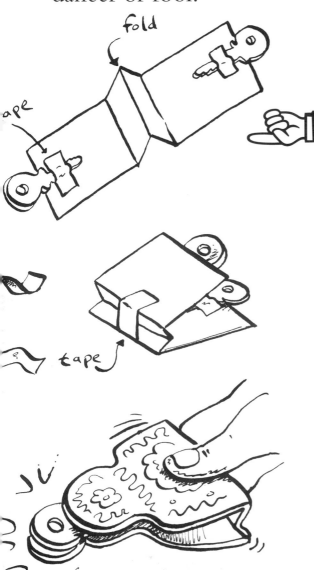

tape

tin lid

Hand Clap

Take a strip of cereal-box card and fold in the middle to create a hinge.
Tape two old flat keys at either end. (You could also use large coins.)

Fold over and put a piece of tape across the hinge.

Trim the card into the shape of Spanish castanets.

19

Sands of Time

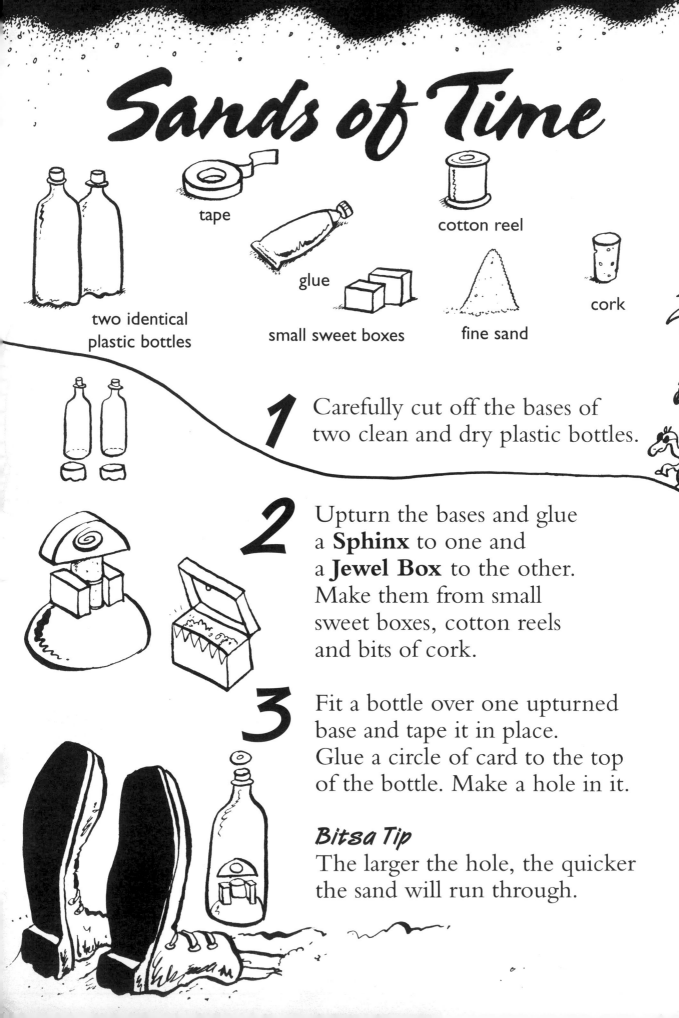

tape

glue

cotton reel

cork

fine sand

two identical
plastic bottles

small sweet boxes

1 Carefully cut off the bases of
two clean and dry plastic bottles.

2 Upturn the bases and glue
a **Sphinx** to one and
a **Jewel Box** to the other.
Make them from small
sweet boxes, cotton reels
and bits of cork.

3 Fit a bottle over one upturned
base and tape it in place.
Glue a circle of card to the top
of the bottle. Make a hole in it.

Bitsa Tip
The larger the hole, the quicker
the sand will run through.

4 Now tape the other bottle in place as shown.
Fill with sand (you may have to sieve it first) and seal with the other base.

By turning the timer upside down the **Sphinx** will be revealed, but her treasure will slowly disappear under the 'Sands of Time'.

Extra Time
Make a set of teeth and see how long it takes to bury them while you clean your own teeth.

Wobbly Hands

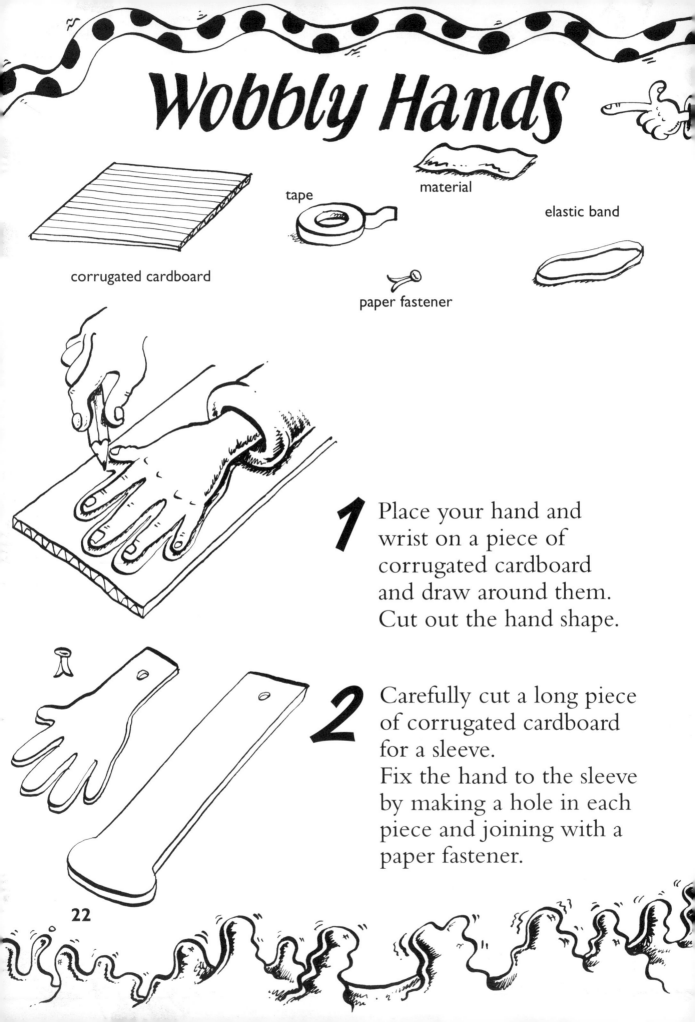

corrugated cardboard

tape

material

elastic band

paper fastener

1 Place your hand and wrist on a piece of corrugated cardboard and draw around them. Cut out the hand shape.

2 Carefully cut a long piece of corrugated cardboard for a sleeve.
Fix the hand to the sleeve by making a hole in each piece and joining with a paper fastener.

3 Cut a long elastic band in two. Tape one length either side of the paper fastener, stretching from the hand to the sleeve.

Cover the sleeve with a piece of material to match your shirt and you are ready to . . .

. . . Do a Wobbly

Hold the cardboard sleeve in your real hand, covered by your shirt sleeve (you could borrow a big mate's jumper) and move your arm up and down.
Create another hand and have two wobbly hands.

Some hand-shakes eh!

Cabinet of Curiosities

large cardboard box

tape

glue

numerous small boxes

washing-up liquid bottle tops

straw

1 Cut one of the small flaps off a cardboard box. Cut the other small flap into a dome shape. Hold it upright with a strip of cardboard.

2 The long flaps will be your doors with plastic washing-up liquid bottle tops for handles.

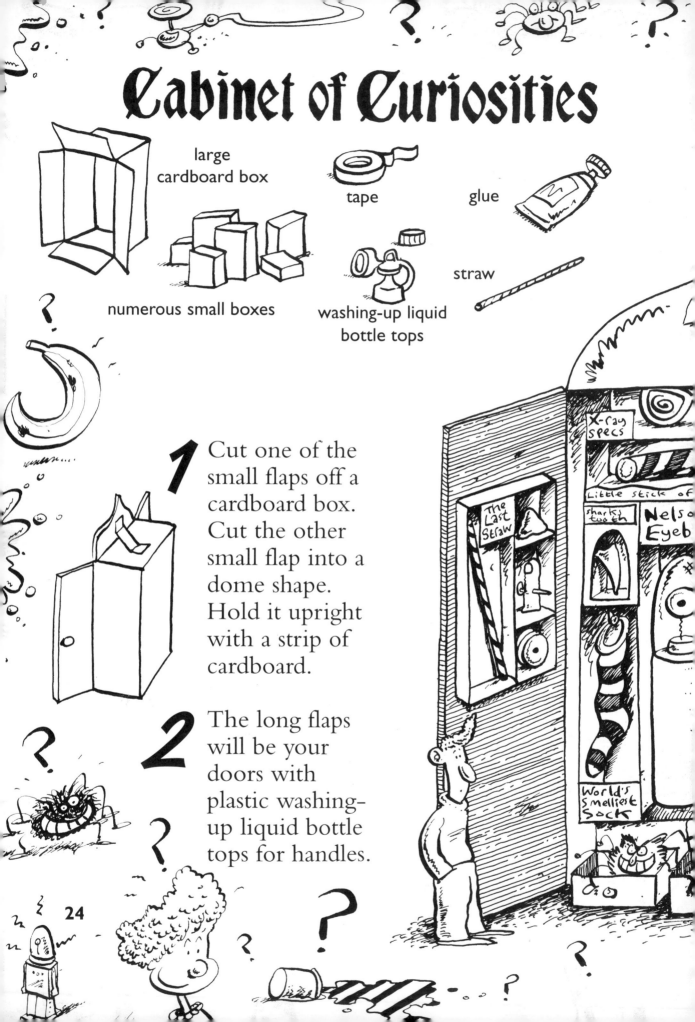

X-ray specs

Little stick of

The Last Straw

sharks tooth

Nels
Eyeb

World's smelliest sock

cardboard shelf

3 Build up various drawers and shelves using empty matchboxes and small boxes. Add bottle tops for handles and cut out some interesting shapes such as arches and domes.

4 Create a secret drawer without a handle, but opened with a straw pushed through a hole in the back.

Start your collection of curious objects and mini Bitsas. They could be small shells, bits of strange-shaped twigs, marbles, even ping-pong balls painted as eyeballs.

Close the doors and hang up your opening times.

k po o l Rocks

100% pure sky

champion conker

the whole tooth

Acrogoats

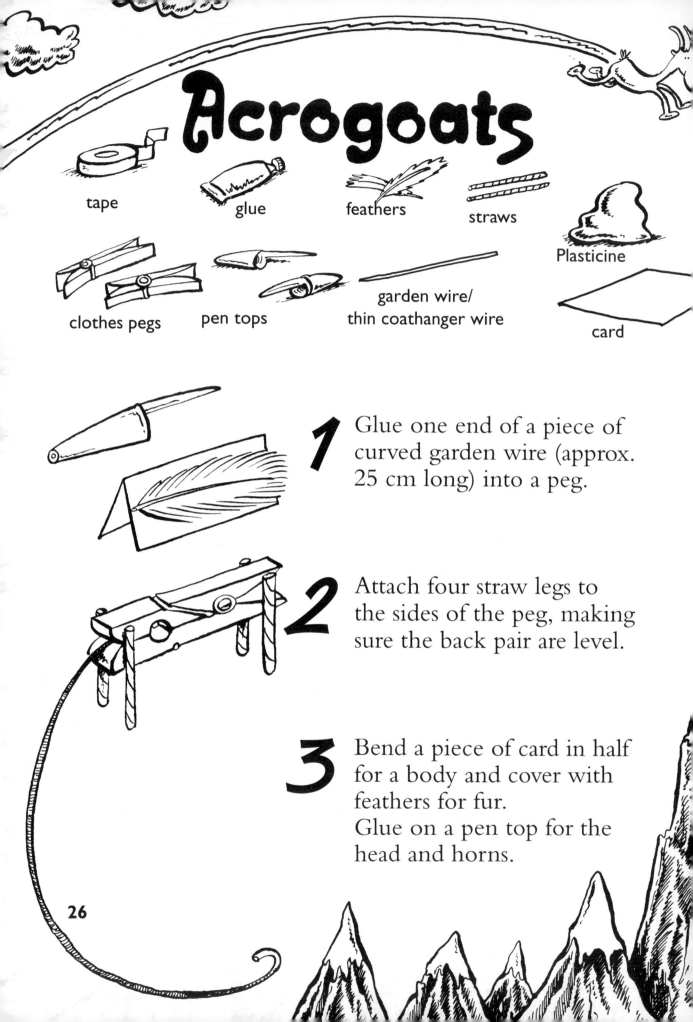

tape

glue

feathers

straws

clothes pegs

pen tops

garden wire/
thin coathanger wire

Plasticine

card

1 Glue one end of a piece of curved garden wire (approx. 25 cm long) into a peg.

2 Attach four straw legs to the sides of the peg, making sure the back pair are level.

3 Bend a piece of card in half for a body and cover with feathers for fur.
Glue on a pen top for the head and horns.

26

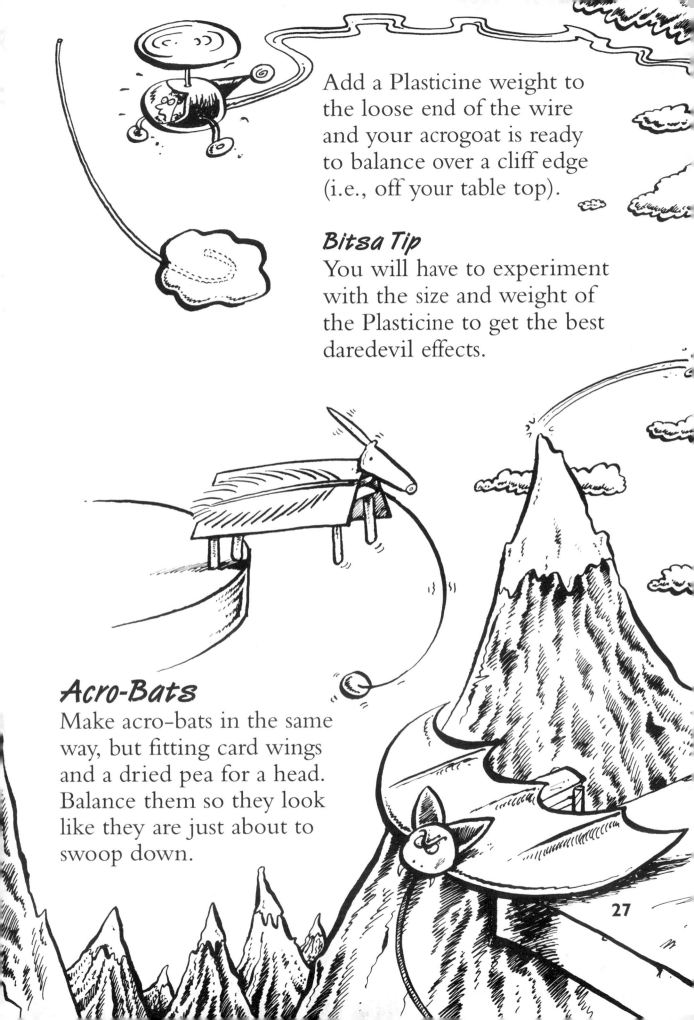

Add a Plasticine weight to the loose end of the wire and your acrogoat is ready to balance over a cliff edge (i.e., off your table top).

Bitsa Tip

You will have to experiment with the size and weight of the Plasticine to get the best daredevil effects.

Acro-Bats

Make acro-bats in the same way, but fitting card wings and a dried pea for a head. Balance them so they look like they are just about to swoop down.

27

Catamaran

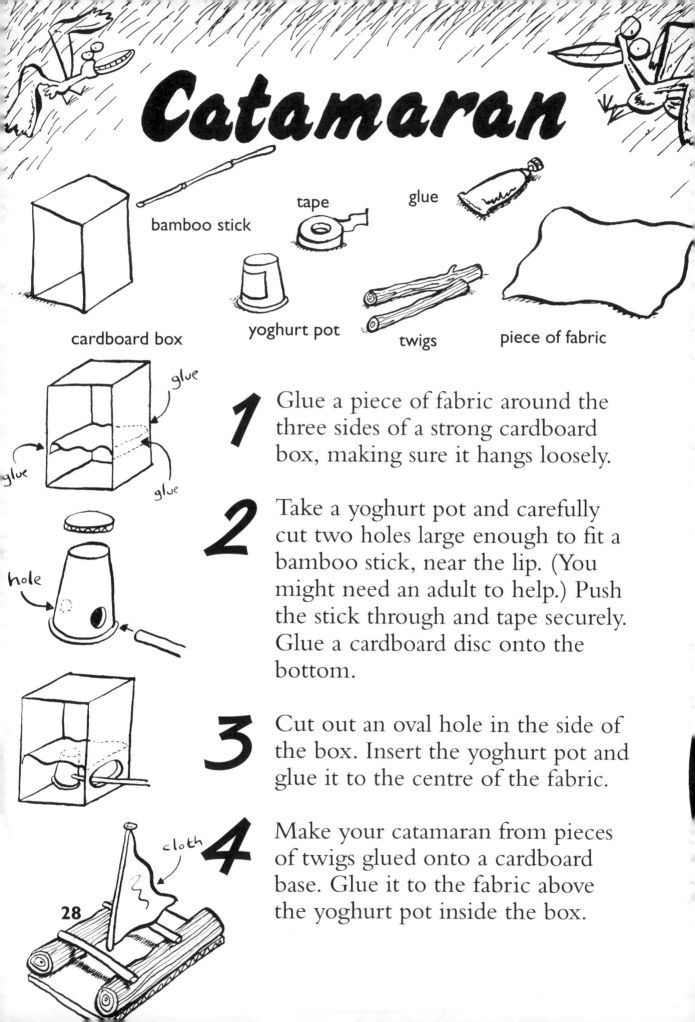

bamboo stick

tape

glue

cardboard box

yoghurt pot

twigs

piece of fabric

1 Glue a piece of fabric around the three sides of a strong cardboard box, making sure it hangs loosely.

2 Take a yoghurt pot and carefully cut two holes large enough to fit a bamboo stick, near the lip. (You might need an adult to help.) Push the stick through and tape securely. Glue a cardboard disc onto the bottom.

3 Cut out an oval hole in the side of the box. Insert the yoghurt pot and glue it to the centre of the fabric.

4 Make your catamaran from pieces of twigs glued onto a cardboard base. Glue it to the fabric above the yoghurt pot inside the box.

5 Paint a stormy seascape around the insides of the box (or paint the scene on paper and then stick it inside the box). You could include a lighthouse, land in the distance – an albatross.
Attach a piece of cardboard to the front with a viewing window.

Bitsa Tip
Cut slits in the top of the box and cover with plastic bags for dramatic lighting effects.

Sailing Instructions
By operating the stick you can turn the catamaran into many sea-sickening positions.

plastic bag strips

Extra Voyage
Change the sailor for a surfer.

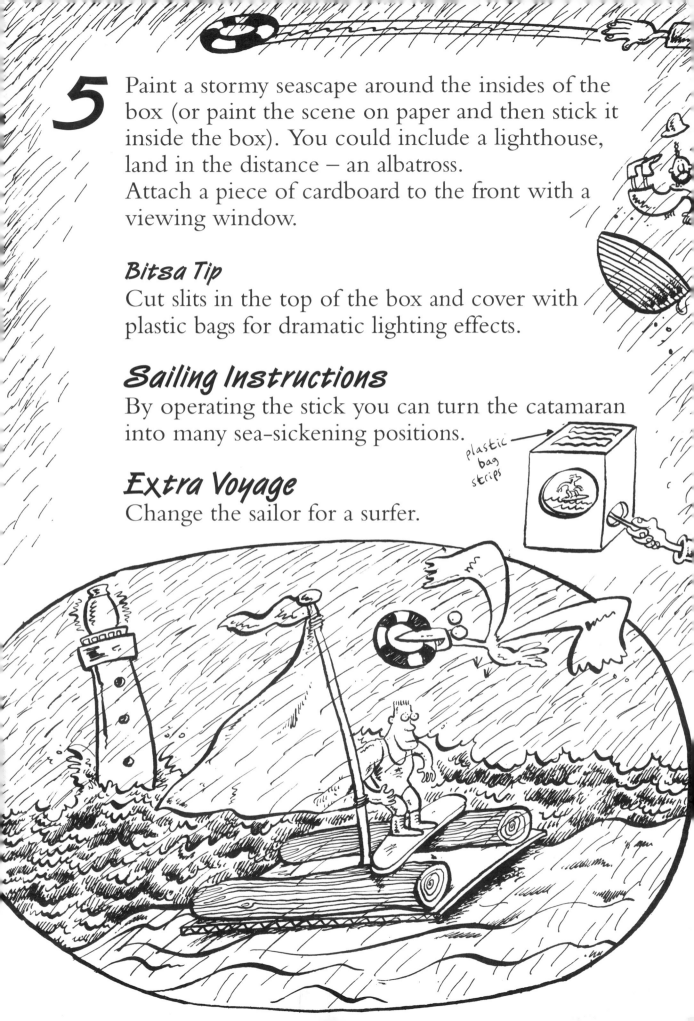

Catflap

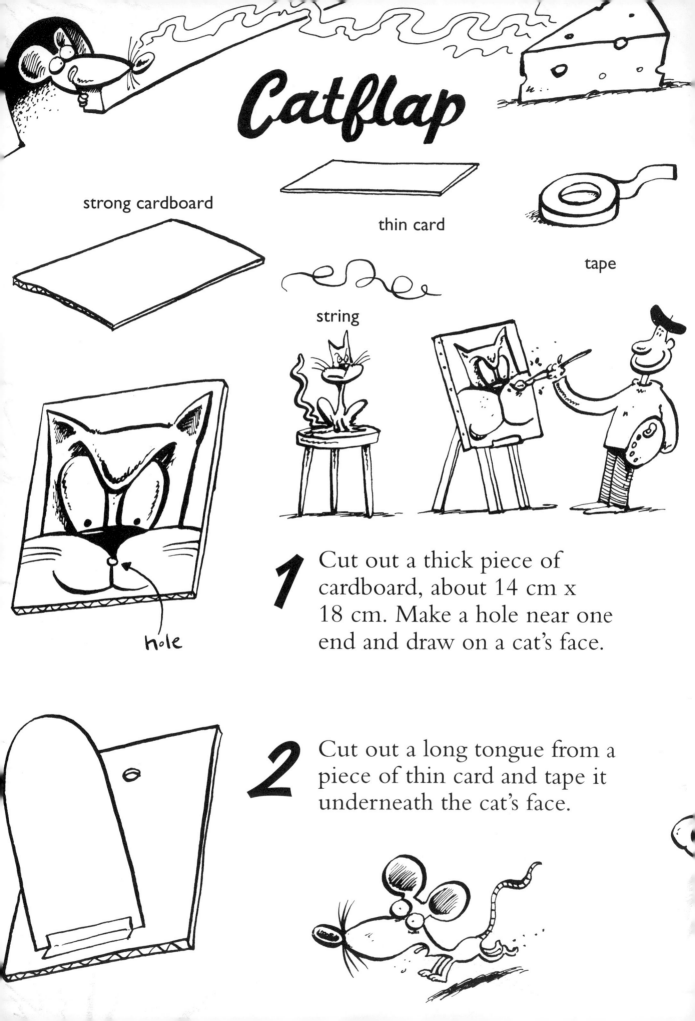

strong cardboard

thin card

tape

string

hole

1 Cut out a thick piece of cardboard, about 14 cm x 18 cm. Make a hole near one end and draw on a cat's face.

2 Cut out a long tongue from a piece of thin card and tape it underneath the cat's face.

3 Tie the string to the bottom of a chair leg. Thread the other end through the hole in the cardboard.

best on carpet

If you pull the string taut with up and down jerk, the cat will flap along the string as if there's a mouse at the end.

Bitsa Tip
For a purr-fect flap, don't pull the string too high, otherwise the head will fall back.

Cat and Mouse
Make another cat and have races to catch mice at the end of the strings.

BITSA

BEATLE BOX

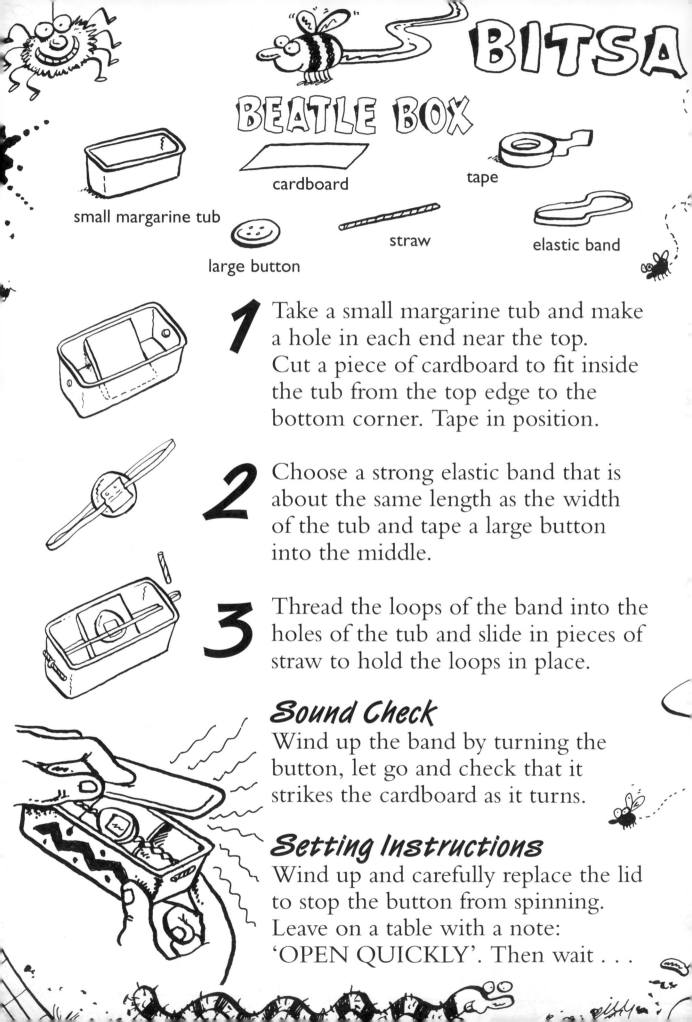

small margarine tub

cardboard

tape

large button

straw

elastic band

1 Take a small margarine tub and make a hole in each end near the top. Cut a piece of cardboard to fit inside the tub from the top edge to the bottom corner. Tape in position.

2 Choose a strong elastic band that is about the same length as the width of the tub and tape a large button into the middle.

3 Thread the loops of the band into the holes of the tub and slide in pieces of straw to hold the loops in place.

Sound Check
Wind up the band by turning the button, let go and check that it strikes the cardboard as it turns.

Setting Instructions
Wind up and carefully replace the lid to stop the button from spinning. Leave on a table with a note: 'OPEN QUICKLY'. Then wait . . .

BUGS
GALLOPING GRASSHOPPERS

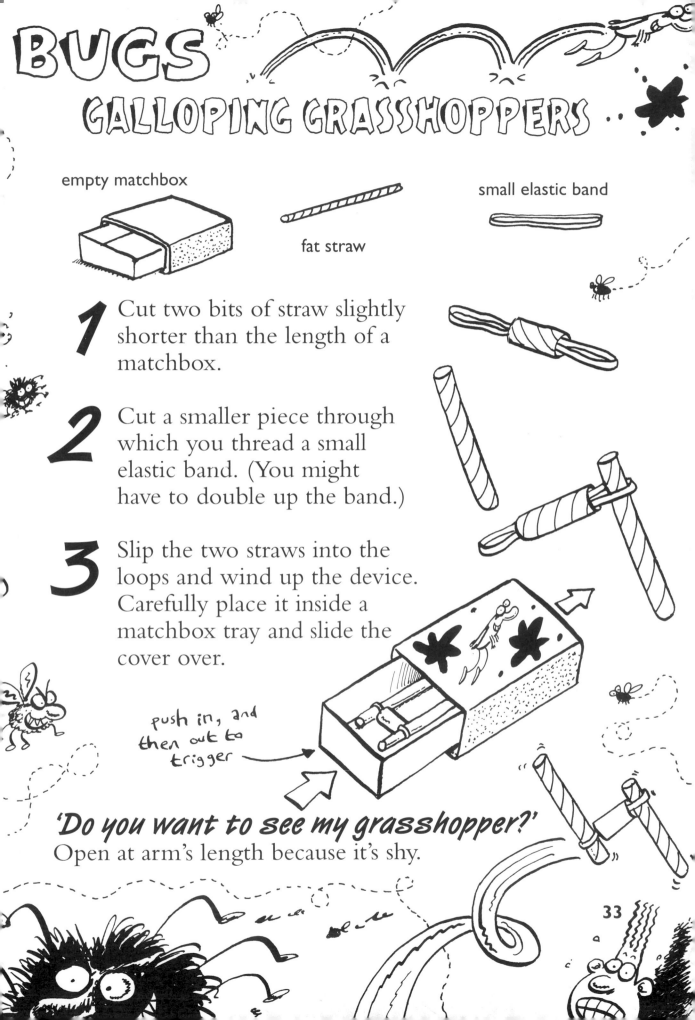

empty matchbox

fat straw

small elastic band

1 Cut two bits of straw slightly shorter than the length of a matchbox.

2 Cut a smaller piece through which you thread a small elastic band. (You might have to double up the band.)

3 Slip the two straws into the loops and wind up the device. Carefully place it inside a matchbox tray and slide the cover over.

push in, and then out to trigger

'Do you want to see my grasshopper?'
Open at arm's length because it's shy.

BITSA BOWL

lots of plastic
juice bottles

various different-shaped
yoghurt or dessert containers

contact glue

PVA glue

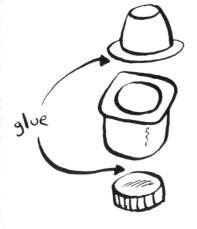

Strike 1 — Bodies

Cover several plastic juice bottles with small strips of newspaper soaked in a watered-down PVA solution. Leave to dry.

Strike 2 — Heads

With a strong contact glue, firmly attach yoghurt pots to the bottle tops.

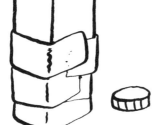

glue

Strike 3 — Cricket Whites

Make caps from other dessert containers, glued upside-down to the yoghurt pots.
Paint on faces and clothes.

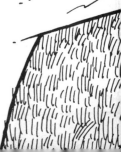

To set up your game, fill each bottle with water. The more you put in, the harder they will be to bowl over.

Bowl 'em Down!

Fit the heads back onto the bottles, arrange them in a row at the end of your room and, with a tennis ball, see how many strikes it takes to bowl them all over.

Extra Strikes

Create different characters such as businessmen, American footballers or head teachers.

HoWzat!

Sunset Lantern

bicycle lamp

tape

cardboard

garden sticks

tissue paper

card

glue

tape

1 Cut a garden stick in three equal lengths using a junior hacksaw. You might need an adult to give you a hand.
Tape the sticks together in a triangle shape.
(If you haven't any sticks you can buy them from garden centres.)

2 Tape a longer stick into each corner. Stand them up and join together at the top.

3 Bow out the sides with two more sets of shorter sticks.

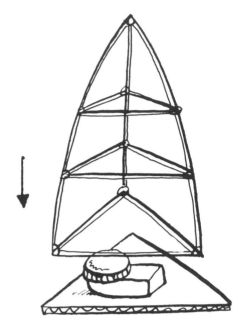

4 Stretch and glue different-coloured tissue paper over your framework.

5 Cut out tropical tree silhouettes from thin pieces of card and attach them to the front. Add a moon and some weird exotic birds.

Spooky Lighting
Switch on the lamp and put it under the lantern. Turn off the bedroom light and marvel at the glow of the evening sun behind the Amazonian forest.

Bitsa Tip
Don't forget to switch off the lamp before you go to sleep!

clouds

parrot

TAPE MEASURE

large cereal packet

two Biro tubes

tape

plastic juice bottles

strong paper

holes

slit

1 Cut two holes in the sides of a large cereal box wide enough to fit a round plastic juice bottle.

2 Make holes in the bottle, either side of the box, so you can slide in two empty Biro tubes.
(You might need an adult to help.)

3 Once the bottle is in place with the Biros slotted in, make up a long length of tape using strips of strong paper stuck together.

BIG   EXTRA B

Draw on various units, either in centimetres, feet or bananas. Attach a plastic clip to the end, made from the corner of a square plastic bottle. This will stop the tape winding through and into the box.

to cut out to make clip

Taping Instructions

Find something or somebody big to measure – a table, a giant sunflower or even your mate's smelly feet.
When finished, wind in the tape using the Biro tube as a handle.
Make a giant pencil to write down the measurements.

card

plastic bottle

The BIG TAPE MEASURE

GINORMOUS   ABSOLUTELY MASSIVE

SKI JUMP

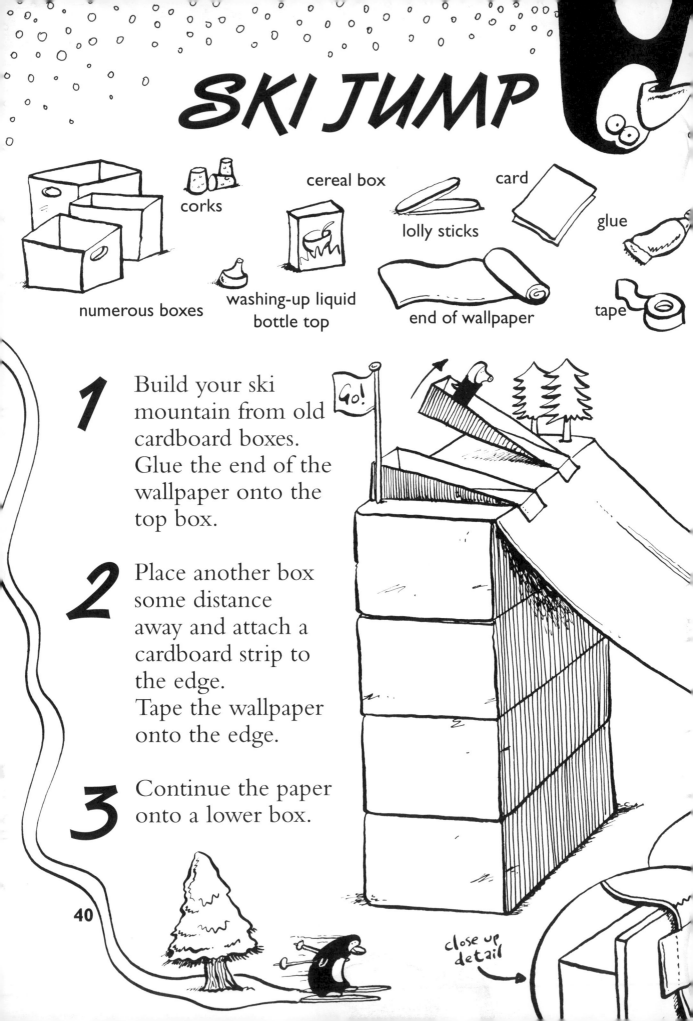

corks

cereal box

card

lolly sticks

glue

numerous boxes

washing-up liquid bottle top

end of wallpaper

tape

1 Build your ski mountain from old cardboard boxes. Glue the end of the wallpaper onto the top box.

2 Place another box some distance away and attach a cardboard strip to the edge.
Tape the wallpaper onto the edge.

3 Continue the paper onto a lower box.

Go!

close up detail

4 The 'start' shutes are made from the corners of a cereal box. Glue the flaps to the edge of the wallpaper.

5 *The Team*

The penguin skiers are made from a cork with two lolly sticks glued onto the bottom. Use card for wings and a plastic washing-up liquid bottle top for the head.

Rules

Place the penguins into their shutes. Raise the ends and watch them speed down the slope, over the jump and land gracefully (or not) at the finish.

flaps

FINISH

41

Forgotten Castle

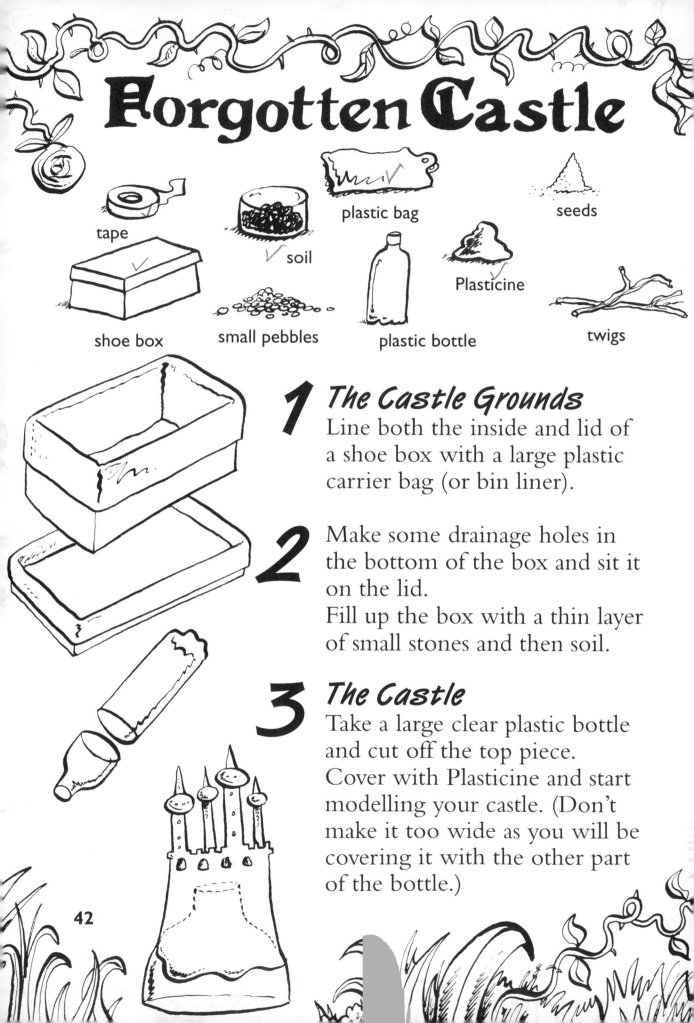

tape

soil

plastic bag

seeds

shoe box

small pebbles

Plasticine

plastic bottle

twigs

1 The Castle Grounds
Line both the inside and lid of a shoe box with a large plastic carrier bag (or bin liner).

2
Make some drainage holes in the bottom of the box and sit it on the lid.
Fill up the box with a thin layer of small stones and then soil.

3 The Castle
Take a large clear plastic bottle and cut off the top piece. Cover with Plasticine and start modelling your castle. (Don't make it too wide as you will be covering it with the other part of the bottle.)

4 Place your cocooned castle into its grounds and create a forest using small twigs, bark, pebbles and moss. You could recycle some weeds from a friend's garden and make a gate from sweet tubes, cardboard and cocktail sticks.

Scatter some grass seeds (bird seed or cress) over the entire forest and water regularly.

Watch daily as the forest completely engulfs 'Sleeping Beauty's Castle' until . . . the prince arrives.

EAZEE TRAPEZEE

two bendy straws

thin card

old magazine/comic

tape

glue

1 Join two straws to each other at the bendy ends by snipping a slit in one end and inserting it into the end of the other. Tape them together.

2 Cut out the figure of a trapeze artist on thin card.
Either draw on a suitable costume or build one up from pictures in an old magazine or comic.
Perhaps the face could be your favourite pop star or politician.

3 Tape the hands onto the trapeze bar.

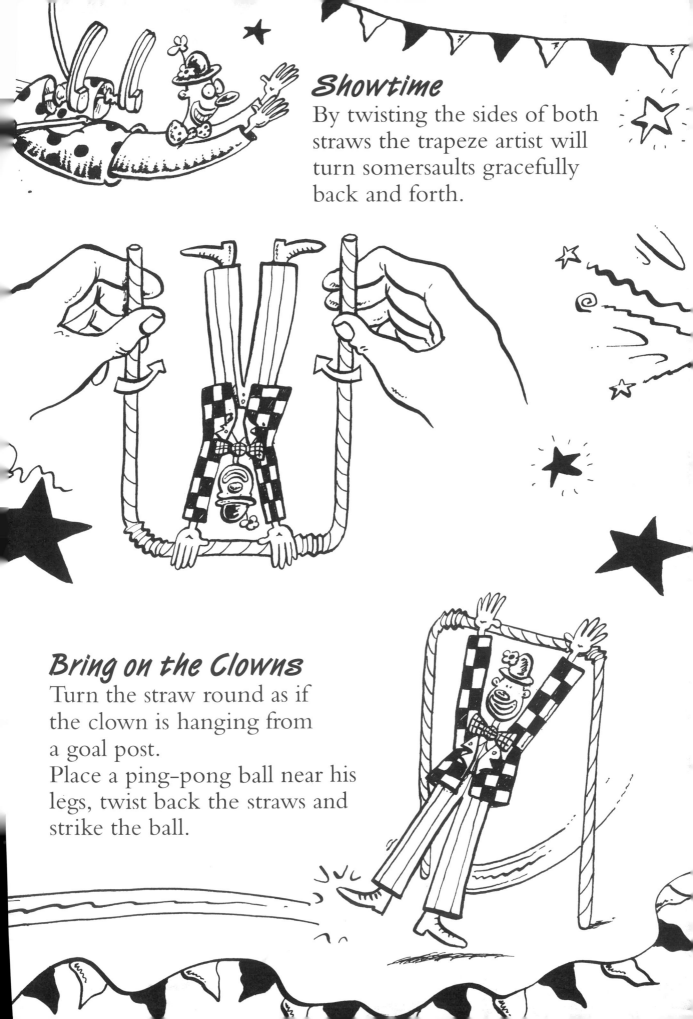

Showtime

By twisting the sides of both straws the trapeze artist will turn somersaults gracefully back and forth.

Bring on the Clowns

Turn the straw round as if the clown is hanging from a goal post.
Place a ping-pong ball near his legs, twist back the straws and strike the ball.

Bitsa Challenge

Next time you invite friends round, ask them to bring as many old boxes, tubes and plastic bottles as they can find.

Lay out the bits in the centre of the room (or out of doors if dry) and sort them into different piles. Number each pile and put these numbers onto scraps of paper.

On another piece of paper make a list of different types of machine – robots, cars, spacecraft, dishwashers, etc. Ask one member of the group to pick three numbers and someone else to choose a machine.

Using just tape, you have five minutes to build a model of . . . say . . . a fork-lift truck. Start the clock!

Marvel at your wonderful creation or disaster. Dismantle it and recycle the bits for another Bitsa Challenge.

Machines:
Dishwasher
Helicopter ✓
Robot ✓
Crane
Car
Rocket ✓
Boat